RESCUED

By

Miriam Newman

DCL Publications, LLC
www.thedarkcastlelords.com

© 2015 Miriam Newman

This book was originally released in 2009 under the title Dancer Dog *by DCL Publications. Some sections of this book have been rewritten and others have been added.*

First Edition August 2015

DCL Publications
1033 Plymouth Dr.
Grafton, OH 44044

ISBN 978-0-9964959-5-0

Cover design by Lynn Hubbard

PUBLISHED IN THE UNITED STATES OF AMERICA

This is book is dedicated to all the tireless, unsung heroes whose daily lives revolve around the endless struggle to save abused, abandoned and unwanted animals who become our forever friends.

It is a true story. Some identities faintly smudged to protect the guilty!

All costs of production have been donated by DCL Publications to benefit Home Free Animal Rescue in Red Bank, New Jersey. Learn more about them at Home Free Animal Rescue on Facebook or www.homefreeanimalrescue.com.

You can find DCL Publications here: www.thedarkcastlelords.com

Find my website and additional books at www.miriamnewman.com

Table of Contents

Chapter One

I was a bereaved person: empty, abandoned, listening for a familiar footstep. In this case, it was the patter of four paws I would miss. Well...no...not a patter, exactly. Polly the Bull Terrier's best gait was a thud. Thud-thud, thud-thud, snuffle, snort, wham. That's the Bull Terrier mamba--one I would never hear again.

My house was too quiet. The television droned inanely, my ancient cat wheezed softly in the rocking chair, undisturbed by the Bull Terrier mamba or a pig-like snout rooting through her cotton-candy fur. Kitty was in Nirvana. I was in hell.

It was Saturday. On Friday, drawn by some inexplicable telepathy, I had gone home to check on Polly. Her heart had been failing for some time--an enlarged, inefficiently pumping bag, which sometimes skipped beats, leading to collapse and unconsciousness in a dog who had been the definition of energy in her day. Sadly, Polly had too few days and Friday was her last. When I came in at lunchtime, she was dead, lying on the living room couch with her head on my favorite throw pillow. She was still warm. I was just moments too late to say goodbye.

That afternoon, my brother came to help bury her. It was a glorious Indian Summer day, just the kind Polly spent as a puppy snoozing under pine trees in the front yard of the old farmhouse where my husband and I lived then. Dave had been enthusiastic about the puppy until the first time she rocketed like an animated bowling ball into his shins, knocking him flat. Bull Terriers do things like that. He hadn't been amused. He also hadn't been well. We knew when we got the pup that Dave had leukemia; he bought her for me so I would have company after he was gone.

Returned to me shortly after his funeral by her breeders, who had kept her at their house when things were at their worst, Polly clung to me as if she knew how much I needed her. I had Dave's fox terrier, Fred, but he was old and deaf and blind--not much company. The little guy felt the same way about me. That dog was my husband's to the end. He lay in bed with Dave for weeks at a time and was there when he drew his last breath. We had to take Fred out of the room so the undertakers could do their job. It broke the poor dog's heart.

Mine wasn't in much better shape. We had lived in the old farmhouse for five years and it felt like mine, but it wasn't. I had money for three months' rent if the landlord kept our deposit— business is business, after all. I had to go and so did the dogs, the cats, and the horses. Dave and I had collected animals the way some people collect shoes and there was no way I was going to see them lose their home just because I was losing mine. Fortunately, my aunt had left me a portion of a sizeable estate, and I humbled myself and called the trust officer, explaining that I was about to be out on the street. I had had major surgery three times in eighteen months while my husband was ill and was in no condition to go job-hunting. It felt like I had been through a war. Sometimes I wakened in the morning unable to remember whether it was morning or night, whether or not Dave was dead. I could barely remember my name.

But Polly was always there, snuffle-snorting and nudging me into some semblance of animation, demanding her breakfast, her walk, her toys. She gave me a reason to get up in the mornings. Polly was a living, breathing hurricane, brimful of wriggling affection. Her slanty little eyes glinted with fun, soliciting even the slightest grunt of laughter, and on most days that was all she got. She didn't care. She was back with me, back where she wanted to be, and all was right with her world.

The trust officer came through and so did the money. I could buy a house. I wasn't picky. It was in the right location, it was the right price, it had enough land for the horses and a garage that could be turned into a small barn. I would never love another house anyway, so if it was structurally sound--I decided--I would take it. Friends and my husband's grown children helped me move. Dave's son, Doug, was going to try his hand at representing his

Dad's dairy brokerage while I held down the office and we would split the proceeds. If that didn't work out, I didn't have many options. I had quit the social services job into which I had been grandfathered without a Master's degree and although everyone conceded I had done it with uncommon skill and dedication for eighteen years, I couldn't go back. But my husband had needed me and that's what you do. "For better, for worse."

Fortunately, I was slowly regaining my health and I had my animals, especially Polly. And then, only a few short years later, I had nothing. The business was defunct. Without Dave, it went South in a hurry and so did Doug and his wife, back to Florida where they had a home they loved. I had taken a secretarial job for a time and several courses towards the degree I now needed, but it was impossible to finish. My aunt's bequest had stretched as far as it could go. I had a living to earn, animals to care for, and I was in my forties. The degree wasn't going to happen and secretarial work didn't thrill me. It didn't pay well, either. When a friend asked me to houseclean for her for extra cash, I didn't say no. Before long, I had more business than I could handle and was turning people away. It was time for a career change…maybe even a mid-life crisis. Dave had died with many of his dreams unfulfilled. I was going to take the time to realize some of mine before time ran out.

And then Polly's time ran out.

* * * *

On Saturday, I called Samantha. We joke that Samantha is my daughter and, in some weird way, it's almost true. She is a much younger friend with whom one of my friends worked. Sam was just a kid then, fresh out of college and struggling to make it on her own. Family problems prevented her from returning home and pretty soon she was in mine. It was an arrangement born of mutual need—I needed income, she needed a room. We liked one another; it was that simple. She loved horses, helped out in the barn, flambee'd her hair making Bananas Foster, entertained me with her romantic entanglements and went to work for the SPCA. She was the one to take Fred there and put him to sleep when his chronic ailments of old age became unbearable and I couldn't stand to do it. Her natural way with animals made her a hit at the shelter, but it didn't pay the bills. She moved on to other things and then marriage. I always say I just got her between the "idges"— college and marriage. But we were close and stayed that way and she was the person I called when I lost Polly.

Sam had stayed close to some other people, too, most of them still working at the shelter. It opened on Sunday at eleven, so we thought maybe the two of us should just go and…well…look. The adoption fee was $90. I had that much in change in a huge vase I kept as a doorstop in the dining room. If I got a puppy on Sunday and rolled my coins Sunday night…and got to the bank on Monday…well, maybe I could go look. I probably wouldn't find anything. I had heard practically every dog in that shelter was a pit bull from an economically depressed area where dog-fighting had become big business. I didn't want one of *those* dogs. Sometimes you could find…well, a small spaniel. An older dog. Some nice little thing that would like to curl up on the couch with me. Right?

Chapter Two

I had forgotten what the local shelter looked like…nearly forgotten where it was. It was a good thing Sam was with me. We drove my pickup and there wasn't much room in the cab for a dog, but I only wanted a small dog and Sam volunteered her lap. She ended up volunteering a lot more than that.

Some of the staff recognized her, so we bypassed the waiting room where a receptionist tried to talk me into taking the one-eyed pug keeping her company. He was little and sweet and the eye didn't bother me. I had a one-eyed horse, too. But I wanted a female. My mother had instilled in me a severe prejudice against male dogs, which she assured me would pee in your house *no matter what*. Fred had convinced me of that, immortalizing himself on my furniture, my saddle, even the slatted wicker clothes hamper and all its contents. Anything that could lift a leg was out.

That eliminated a number of dogs. There were very young puppies that looked like Shepherd-Collie mix, but I dreaded housebreaking. I hadn't slept through a night for years while Dave was ill. Getting an older dog might mean I could get some sleep, I thought.

A few dogs refused to engage with us, but most came straight to the front of their pens, paws and noses pressing the diamond-shaped cyclone mesh, eyes intent. *"Take me, take me!"* those eyes pleaded. *"Get me out of this place!"* The shelter was well-run, well-managed and scrupulously clean. But it was a typical November day, sullen and cold. Chill permeated every inch of a concrete-and-wire environment where doggie doors opened onto outdoor kennel runs and a stiff breeze wafted in with every trip made by every dog. It was freezing and smelled of disinfectant, and the din of all those dogs never ceased. A few poor animals had tails bandaged because they beat them endlessly against the cement in a frantic bid for attention—anyone's— anything to get them out into the world again. They were prisoners who had committed no crime.

Most were pit bulls. I couldn't help being drawn to them because Polly had been a Bull Terrier, a separate breed, but with some of the same traits. They were almost desperately friendly, as though aware of their reputation and out to win friends at any cost. I just shook my head.

"What about a mix?" Sam asked. "Some of them aren't pure pit."

"I don't know," I said, dubiously. "That blood predominates." The face certainly predominated. Everywhere I looked, I saw the broad foreheads, wide-set eyes and powerful jaws of fighting dogs. All of these dogs had been tested for temperament, but that breed is nothing for the faint-hearted to take on. Of course, I wasn't faint-hearted. I was used to handling twelve-hundred-pound horses. "Let's keep looking."

Halfway down the first side, a young brindle bitch came to greet us. She stood up against the wire with such grace and such delicate feet that I knew at once she was a pit mix. She had the face, but thinner. Thin was the operative word for that dog. They could not have had her long and she must have been in atrocious shape when she came in, judging by the number of ribs and vertebrae still visible.

Sure enough, "I'm a stray," read the placard on the front of her pen. But such a sweet stray. There were white patches, like little eyes, on the backs of her paws. They twinkled as she moved, like a light show, and her walk...I had never seen anything like it. Accustomed to watching the movement of horses, I saw at once that she didn't walk in a four-beat gait, but in a lateral movement like a pacer.

"What the heck is she?" I asked Sam. "Hound?" My friend just shrugged, as mystified as I was, while the little bitch tried to inhale her fingers. She gave me a courteous nosing, too, as I trailed my hand along the wire. The poor thing had a sizeable wart in the middle of her forehead and she fell right on it, overbalancing when she tried to follow us past the corner of her pen. I could feel her eyes boring into my back as we left her.

Still, I checked every pen: every one, both sides, all occupants. When we got to the last one, I turned. Sam was watching me as if trying hard not to laugh.

"That one," I said, pointing back at the brindle.

She just nodded. "Oh, yeah."

They had a "get acquainted" room at the shelter and I asked that they put a cat in there. I had two old, defenseless cats.

"Oh, she won't bother them," the young kennel technician leading in my prospective dog assured us. "Dancer is a sweetheart." The shelter had a policy of naming every dog that came in and I could see how the little bitch had earned her sobriquet. She greeted each human with her forepaws, conveniently offered at waist level. She touched you like a feather, only asking if you were interested, and she had misty, melting eyes and the cutest streak of white from chin to chest which showed to full advantage in the greeting position. Most people were interested and I was no exception. Still, I wanted to see if she would eat the cat.

She didn't spare him a glance. He was a dead ringer for Kitty, too, right down to his semi-comatose state. That cat never moved the entire time we were in the room and Dancer treated him like he was invisible. After her initial greeting, she treated Sam and me the same way. She was just a nose on four legs, investigating every object in the room with almost desperate intensity, as though she had been so long deprived of any sensory input meaningful to a dog that she was stocking up. My eyes filled and I grabbed a tissue, intercepting a puzzled look from the technician.

"My dog just died on Friday," I blubbered, though that wasn't the only reason I was crying. "She had heart failure." I didn't want the girl to think I had been negligent in any way and I hadn't. I had dosed Polly with digitalis, Lasix, L-Carnitine—anything the might extend her life span, all in vain. Bags and cans of her expensive prescription diet littered my back kitchen. I should donate them to some vet hospital, I thought. Maybe the one that had performed her echocardiogram, where the vet had looked at me with compassion and told me I could do all these things, but my dog was still going to die.

"What kind was it?" the technician asked sympathetically.

"A Bull Terrier."

"Really?" she asked, looking at me with new respect. Bullies were notoriously hard to handle. "Then you might be a good person to take a pit mix."

"Maybe." I watched the bitch circling the room, ignoring us in favor of the good smells. "What's she mixed with?"

"Probably whippet. She's five or six months old and weighs twenty-nine pounds. She should mature at about forty-five."

I glanced at Sam. "The perfect size." I had been raised with hunting dogs—setters and retrievers—and although I had thought I needed a little dog because I had a little house, 45 pounds sounded a lot more pleasing. Polly had been just slightly larger and Polly had been built like a brick wall. This dog with her tiger-striped coat showed a lot of whippet. Her body would be svelte even after she gained weight and she had the elegant, curved tail of the whippet and the soft "rose" ears you see in that breed. Nothing ever got rid of the pit bull face, but she had a very sweet expression. Whippets were gentle dogs, the conscientious objectors of dogdom. Surely that would overcome much of Dancer's fighting blood.

"I don't suppose she's housebroken?" I ventured.

"Probably not," the technician admitted. "She was on the street and then here. But she's very intelligent. If you crate her, she shouldn't be a problem."

"I have a crate," I said, feeling more and more confident. She was old enough to sleep through the nights. "I think I'd like to take her."

Sam beamed. No matchmaker making shiddoch was ever happier. While the technician took the dog back to prepare her, we went to the receptionist's office so they could call the vet for a reference. My vet's office was at her home and she was usually there on Sundays. I knew she wouldn't mind being bothered for this happy event.

All my good feelings evaporated in an instant. My vet's phone didn't answer. It didn't switch to a tape or a service, it just didn't answer. At all. The receptionist's expression changed as quickly as my mood. She thought we were trying to put one over on her.

"I know that's the number," I insisted. "I called it a hundred times while my dog was sick. Can you try again?"

She tried again. Nothing. She hung up with a look of increasing exasperation.

"I'm sorry. We can't release the dog without a vet's reference. She'll have to stay here until we get one. If she's still available at that time, you can try again." Her expression suggested frozen tundra. No way was she going to hold that dog for me.

"I'll be right back," Sam said. While we waited, assuming she was going to the rest room, she marched straight into the shelter manager's office. He was a personal friend of hers and had been to my house, seen my dog and met me. He knew where Dancer would be going and it wasn't that easy getting someone to take a pit bull, even a mix. Within moments, he was in the office signing in place of the vet, issuing papers to us over the furious glare of his receptionist. She handed me the leash and a bag of dog chow without a word, pocketing my check like it was blood money.

"I'll give her a very good home," I promised. She didn't answer.

"Bitch," Sam muttered as we exited, and I didn't pretend to think she was talking about my new dog.

Chapter Three

I had been so unsure of my intention to get a dog that I hadn't taken a leash, and the little nylon loop they gave us at the shelter didn't afford much control. Dancer gave me a whirlwind tour of the parking lot.

"For twenty-nine pounds, she sure can pull," I commented, just missing a close encounter of the worst kind with a telephone pole. "She peed three times. Let's go."

Sam slid into the passenger's seat, snapped her fingers, and the dog launched herself up and into her lap.

"She can jump, too," I observed.

There were no more calisthenics after that. The dog circled once and curled up in a neat little package in Sam's lap, burying her nose in the crook of her arm. She didn't move.

"She's probably afraid we're going to take her back," I said.

Sam nodded. "Yeah, she can't believe her luck."

It certainly looked that way, because the dog didn't budge during the entire ride home. I could hear her breathing gustily, with her nose squashed against Sam's elbow, but there was no movement. She didn't barf, either. Polly had always let fly any contents in her stomach before I reached the first cross-street, but this dog looked like a good traveler.

Dancer finally raised her head when she heard the crunch of gravel beneath my tires.

"We're home," I said in that tone you use when you give a dog the good news, and her soft ears pricked. She sat up, looking eagerly out the window. She hadn't come to any palace, just a hundred-year-old Victorian cottage swamped with evergreens, bamboo and a lot of weeds I never got time to whack. But it boasted a fascinating yard I had already decided to have fenced despite the cost. Sam and I walked the perimeter of the proposed yard so the dog could pee copiously once more, and then my friend had to take her leave of us. She had been walking Dancer and the dog seemed a trifle confused when I took the leash, as though she had considered Sam her new owner, but when I led her into a warm place that smelled like food, she went right in.

Kitty, accustomed to dogs, actually deigned to thump down from the rocking chair to greet us. The next thing I knew, I was flattened against the solid oak door as a rampaging whirlwind ripped out of my unprepared grasp. The cat had *MOVED*—God save the mark!—and Dancer responded instantly. Poor Kitty, who hadn't run that fast since her youth, whipped up the slippery wooden steps. She was able to make good her getaway because

Dancer had never before encountered steps. The dog thrashed at the bottom, lunging in impotent fury, unable to deduce how to get upstairs.

"No!" I admonished when I could catch my breath. "Bad dog! No chase!"

She looked at me as if I was crazy.

"Oh, come on," I relented. "Let's eat."

"*I was just about to,*" her expression said. "*Where did that cat go, anyway?*"

Kitty had gone to the attic. She stayed there for a long time and she must have had telepathy with Smudgie, the barn cat, because I didn't see old Smudge for days.

Her food disappeared and so did she.

There followed a delightful afternoon and evening of snoozing on the couch with the dog tucked in the same position she had assumed with Sam, in this case flat on top of me with her nose between my neck and shoulder. As long as her eyes were hidden, that tuck seemed to say, she couldn't spot anyone coming to take her away from heaven. A wave of protective warmth suffused my heart. This dog must have been through hell. Who knew what awful things had happened to her? Well, her troubles were over. I would see to that.

Dancer ate well, she peed well every two hours on the dot, and she looked at the crate into which I proposed to put her that night. She looked. That wasn't the same as going inside. Going inside is the one thing she didn't do: not for food, not for toys, not for any reason whatsoever. She just looked at me with the same expression she had worn when I told her not to eat the cat. "*You're crazy,*" that look said. "*I just got out of one of those things, only bigger.*"

At bedtime, I finally pushed her reluctant little rump into the crate. Gently. I gave her a chewy toy, I said goodnight and went upstairs.

She didn't cry or howl. She didn't bother. Ten minutes later I heard something that sounded like a King Kong escaping from his steel cage on the pier in New York. The dog was trying to kill her crate. It looked like she might kill herself in the process, so I let her out, carried her upstairs, spread a beach towel on the bed in case of accidents and put her up. She curled into a perfect little ball and spent the rest of the night in peaceful slumber if you didn't count her walking on my head every two hours as she circumnavigated her way to the window over the bed. It was her way of telling me she needed to go out. Every two hours. All night. All bloody night.

At seven o'clock, I staggered out of bed in time to intercept Dancer's attempt to relieve herself in the corner of the dining room. "No!" I admonished. "Bad dog. You do that outside. Out. *OUT!*"

She stood up in mid-pee and trotted to the door and never peed in the house again. Well, almost never.

There was a very nice pen with cyclone fence and a comfy doghouse next to the hayshed and that is where I put the dog while I fed the horses and mucked out their stalls. Noises like those of a caged tiger kept interrupting my train of thought, but I soldiered on. She would not get out of that pen. It had been built to hold a Bull Terrier. I would not encourage her by speaking to her; she would just have to get used to the routine.

Thirty nerve-wracking minutes later, it was back into home-sweet-home and crate-not-so-sweet-crate. It took a bit more of a push to get her in this time, but I persisted. I knew you should never force a dog into a crate and I was really sorry I didn't have more time to acclimate her, but figured once I was out of the house and she wasn't getting attention, she'd settle down. I was only going to be gone two hours. I really didn't have a choice. There were dangers in that house about which a stray from a kennel knew nothing. I had to crate her because it was safer. She would be all right.

Sure enough, when I unlocked the front door two hours later, I was met by peace and quiet. There was no whining, no barking, no mad banging on the crate. That was because she wasn't in it.

She was on the couch. The barred door of the shipping-style crate had been pulled backwards into the interior with such force that it would take a crowbar to get it out again and the crate would never be really usable. Which was just as well, because I never did use it. When I had to go out that afternoon, I left the dog on the couch and returned to exemplary order. She had not gone to the bathroom, she had not chewed anything (the cat was still in the attic, of course) and my dog was very happy to see me. Once she got her own way, Dancer was the soul of courtesy.

On Tuesday, after her phone jack that had been removed by her children was plugged back in, Dr. N. came to meet Dancer. The doctor's office was not yet finished and she made house calls. That was fine with the dog, who proceeded to charm the socks off both the vet and her assistant. She spent her exam time on the couch, kissing everyone. Nothing bothered her: not being probed, weighed, injected, not even having blood drawn. Dr. N. left, pronouncing my dog "a good one." Of course, she hadn't seen the crate. I had hidden it in the back kitchen.

A friend loaned me another one, all wire this time. "Of course the poor dog was terrified," Nancy said. "It's dark as the tomb in one of those shipping crates. Give her something that lets in light."

Well, my dog was a good one. I put her in the larger, lighter, altogether more suitable wire crate and went to work for the afternoon.

She wasn't howling when I came in this time and she was still in her crate. So were bits of her teeth and some of her toenails, lying in small pools of blood on the floor of the crate. Several of the wires were seriously bent, though they had held fast.

"Oh-my-God," I said in a tone of horrified awe. I let her out. Her bloody paws seemed not to bother her one bit and she gave me many slobbery, bloody kisses, licking away my tears.

Dancer spent her subsequent days on the couch, listening to the sounds of my friends Ed and Dave putting up a fence in the yard. I noticed that she was not quite as delighted to meet men as she was to greet women. As a matter of fact, I kept her away from Ed, who was large and dark-haired. Dave, small and blond, seemed to be more acceptable. Still, they were men and she didn't particularly like them.

Well, was she in for a shock. I ran out of dog food and a few other things and had to go to the store and I already knew she rode well in the truck, so I decided to take her along. I wasn't about to leave her in the truck while I shopped, because Polly had chewed the knob off the gearshift lever in my other truck when I did that. Instead, I took Dancer to stay with my brother and his wife in the motel they managed. If there was one man who was good with dogs, it was my brother. This would be kill or cure, I decided.

My sister-in-law, Bertie, and her helper, Rhonda, came

across the parking lot to see the dog. Dancer, who had never uttered a threatening noise, suddenly made one. It was ugly and it meant business. That truck was my home, she was guarding me, and she wasn't going to let them near. It was the first time I fully realized I had a pit bull—a dog that would give its life for me without hesitation.

"Uh, we'll get out," I squeaked. "Honestly, she's never like this. I don't know what got into her."

I knew what had gotten into her. Secure in her attachment to me, the dog had appointed herself my protector. *"No!"* I hissed. *"Mine! No bite!"* Once out of the truck, she offered her paws to the two women without hesitation, went into the motel like the Queen making an entrance, and charmed everyone in the lobby. They were all women. A woman came in to register—a woman who clearly liked dogs—and Dancer wriggled up to her with her whippet tail wringing in friendly circles. She had a drink of water. She had biscuits. She nearly had a heart attack when my brother walked in.

"Leave this to me," he said, taking her leash. "Go do your shopping." I fled with one last guilty look—off to buy kibble, collar, all the things I hadn't bought yet because I hadn't been sure I was going to get a dog. Well, I had one now. I just hoped I would still have a brother when I returned.

I tiptoed back into the motel lobby with trepidation, afraid of what I might see. What I saw was a man sitting on a couch with a dog asleep on his lap. I have never known what Richard did and he never told me, but from that day on Dancer was no longer afraid of men.

Chapter Four

Dancer began to feel at home. Very much at home. Eventually the cat came out of the attic and when Dancer attempted to ingest her, I used the tried-and-true method employed with Bull Terriers. One could not be wimpy with those dogs. Pinning Dancer to the wall, I gave her a hard shake, screaming, *"No! Mine! No touch!"* Then I gave her head a distinct smack into the wood paneling for good measure and turned her loose, first checking to see that Kitty had a clear path to run. Dancer shook her head and looked at me as much as if to say, *"Why didn't you just tell me?"* That was the end of chasing Kitty.

They began sleeping together. I would come home to the sight of the two of them curled up like old friends on the couch. But, eventually, that began to pall on the still-young dog.

I kept the attic door open for Kitty, on a safety chain that permitted just enough room for a cat to slip through. She loved it up there and it was a refuge if the dog forgot her manners. Soon Dancer apparently began to wonder what made that such an attractive place. She bulled her way through the chain and went to find out.

I returned home in the late afternoon. Dancer had long since learned to negotiate the stairs, down which warm golden sunshine was beaming. Things were twinkling in that sunlight— things that had been in the attic. Paper. Ribbon. Tinsel. Christmas ornaments, some of them ground to powder. Draped in graceful profusion, they assumed a rough Christmas-tree shape, artfully decorating my steps. I couldn't help it; I started to laugh. Dancer had been standing at the top of the stairs with her ears pinned, unsure of my reaction, but she launched into a full charge, leaping into my arms in a state of sheer delight. She thought I was pleased. That laugh cost me, big time.

From then on, she greeted me with some chewed item every time I returned. It was a gift, her thanks to me for the food, soft bed, warmth and cuddling. She never understood why I wasn't grateful. If I was too upset, she chewed more things in a bid to regain my good will. I reopened the wire crate and acclimated her to it—again. This time, I took the time to drape it and put in a soft bed and some really, really attractive things—knuckle bones. Dancer would go in the crate for knuckle bones and eventually she would even let me close the door. I began to feel some hope for my house. I left her in there with bones for ten minutes…then fifteen…finally half an hour. At last, half a day. All was well. I cornered the local market on knuckle bones and left my rapidly-fattening dog on provender while I went to work.

When I came back, she was still chewing contentedly. Pleased and vastly relieved, I let her out.

With all of her energy unexpended, Dancer decided to demonstrate what the homecoming dance really entailed. Her tail did the demo. It beat, lashed, practically whirled in a frantic tempo of delight…whipped into corners and against door jambs, slashing like a knife. It had the same effect as a knife, too, on the dog. A spray of blood began flying in time with her tempestuous welcome, a million shining droplets over every wall, window, and piece of furniture. There was blood on the mirrors, on the lamps, and on my face.

"Stop!" I screamed frantically. Encouraged by my reaction, Dancer increased the tempo. A shower of red coated the television screen and the curtains. She was ramping up. "God, stop it!" I gasped, leashing her in mere seconds so I could get her out into the open where she would stop beating her tail on things. She swiped the pillars on the porch, but then we were pretty much in the clear and I could look at the tip of her tail. It looked like hamburger.

Oh, whippets always did that when they were young, my friend Nancy told me. When things were calmer, I called her because I needed to talk. Her parents had bred whippets, she said, and their house always looked like the scene of an axe murder. The dog would catch on before too much longer and stop injuring herself. She advised buying sponges, not for the dog, but for my walls.

I did buy some sponges and I didn't put up a Christmas tree that year. I come from a mixed Irish-Jewish family and am accustomed to a double set of holidays being observed, but apparently that year the God of Abraham was making some sort of a statement. There was nothing to put on the tree.

Christmas Eve was a little subdued that year, but fortunately I was invited to a party at the home of a husband and wife veterinarian team. I had gone to an office party at the place where I had done secretarial work and where they had been nice enough to invite me back for the festivities, so I was wearing burgundy velvet and pearls, the most expensive pair of pantyhose I had ever purchased, and new shoes. I looked great. Returning from Party #1 in a state of bonhomie, anxious to let the dog out and get to Party #2, I flew into my house.

The crate was upside down. The dog was right side up with her bed on top of her, but she couldn't seem to move. Panicked, I opened the door and tried to get my dog out, but it didn't work because her tail was pinned between the wire and the floor. She had completely rolled the crate, pinning her tail and nearly severing it. With the superhuman strength of adrenaline pouring through my body, I was able to upend the heavy crate with the dog inside and free her. She shot out like a cannonball, battered tail whipping. This time, blood flew all the way to the ceiling. My burgundy velvet was quickly soaked with scarlet; my legs looked like someone had beaten me. So did my face. Eventually, somehow, I got Dancer out the door and let her pee and then brought her back inside, where I wrapped paper towels around her tail in a bid to soak up some of the blood so I could assess the damage. It was bad. Where was I going to find someone to stitch up a dog on Christmas Eve?

I had underestimated my friends. In a voice cracking somewhere between a laugh and a sob, I phoned my hostess to tell her why I wouldn't be making an appearance.

"Oh, no problem," Lady Doc said. "Bring the dog. My husband will stitch her up."

The only clean clothes I had were jeans and sweaters, so that's what I wore to the party. Doc's wife spent her time sponging blood out of my hair while he was repairing the dog and then it was on with the show. Dancer was a hit, begging treats from everyone while her tail, heavily encased in Vet-Wrap, beat a tattoo on the walls.

Many gin and tonics later, I drove the considerable distance home praying we would not run into any police cars, because I probably would have run into a police car or anything else that got in my way. I had never driven in that condition and never have done it since, but I was desperate. Dancer had driven me to drink.

Chapter Five

In my cozy little barn which once had been a garage, I had three horses: mine and two boarders, kept to give my horse company and cover the cost of maintaining him. If I had to name the three most expensive sports I can think of—just off the top of my head—I would name yachting, golf and having a horse. And I, the woman who had to roll coins to buy a dog for ninety dollars, owned a horse.

I didn't want Dancer anywhere near those horses. She had the heart of a lion, but the legs of a gazelle—long, slender and fragile. They were whippet legs. I had a friend whose whippet was kicked by a horse and had a leg so badly injured that it proved fatal, which is pretty rare in this age of animal orthopedic surgeons. That wasn't happening to my dog.

Since she hated the pen, I began leaving Dancer in my newly-fenced yard. I had bought her a warm coat, since she shivered violently in the winter weather, and she had a well-padded dog house, pine trees for shelter, and my proximity at the barn. If she began to whine, I could return and put her inside the house.

She never whined. She never gave me any warning at all, unless it was the earth-moving sound I heard coming from under the tubular steel gate. Before I could even make the short hop to the lawn, Dancer had joined me at the barn, grinning in doggy delight. "*Boy, that was fun,*" her grin seemed to say. "*Where else can I dig?*" Her Fu-Manchu toenails had made short work of the frozen ground beneath the gate, which is where I found her expensive coat hanging. She had scraped it off as she slipped through a dog-sized depression, testimony to her earnest excavation.

"OK, fool," I said, strapping her coat back on. "I hope you can outrun the suckers." With those fond words, I picked up the handles of the wheelbarrow and resumed my thankless task. Forking fifty pounds of manure into the tipsy conveyance, I cursed as I tried not to catch its wheel in frozen hoof prints that stretched in an endless sea reaching from barn to manure pile. Eventually, I gave up and took the stuff out by hand in muck tubs, teetering in the peaks and valleys of the frozen wasteland with those same fifty pounds in my hands, trying to get to the pile before I lost my footing. The chore was just as bad when the ground thawed. Then, it sucked my boots off.

Another dog might have eaten the manure; most dogs did. Another dog might have followed its warm, reeking trail and wallowed in the pile. Another dog might have...no, no matter.

Dancer was not another dog. She was Miss Fastidious. The Teflon Princess. She repelled dirt. Bedded down on fresh wood chips in the cleanest corner she could find, she gave me a reproachful stare. *The things I do for you*, it said. Sighing, she put her chin on her front paws and watched me. And watched me. The dog never closed her eyes. Her ears were at the alert. She was tracking me like radar.

Our pattern was set. I mucked while she watched. As the weather grew colder and she was unable to tolerate the elements, even inside the barn, I pulled the truck into the space next to the barn and let her sit in the cab. I put a quilt in the passenger seat and occasionally ran the heater for brief periods and the dog sat there, ramrod straight, eyes glued to me. The barn was a shed-row style and opened directly onto the pasture so the horses could come and go at will. Unfortunately, many times the place seemed to exert some sort of magnetic attraction, which drew them the minute I set foot in it. They wouldn't leave me alone and I spent a lot of time shouting, sometimes because they came in at a dead run and nearly killed me.

Dancer had found her purpose in life. She had no herding blood in her pedigree and no inclination to herd the horses; she simply faced them off, unless I had put her in the truck. If she was loose, she described an arc around me that was sacred ground. Any horse trying to cross that area would do it only over her dead body and I was afraid they would, but they were intimidated. If she was in the truck, she gave vocal warning--a throaty *ROO-ROO-ROO* that meant, "*Heads up, they're coming!*" Forewarned in that manner, I had at least a fighting chance.

Rats that had been digging cavernous holes in the floors of my stalls had no chance at all. Dancer killed them like the half-terrier she was, dispatching them instantly with a savage shake of the head that snapped their necks like toothpicks. Ground hogs and moles were on her hit list. The dog could dig like a machine, shredding any roots that impeded progress the same way she killed rats, with the same violent shake of her head. I learned to unplug the electric fence any time she was with me, because she would bolt straight through it--screaming in pain--in pursuit of anything that ran.

I knew a family of foxes lived in the deep woods behind my pasture. They liked to cross my property and then go over the road into a cornfield where mice and other tasty treats awaited them. The big dog fox usually preceded his mate and young ones. One Sunday morning when the foxhunt had gone elsewhere and Sir Fox was escorting the wife and kids out to eat, he made the mistake of trying to take the shortcut he had created because Polly and I never bothered him. He didn't know there had been a changing of the guard.

There was no "*ROO-ROO-ROO*" that morning; there was

no sound at all. Silent, deadly and running at very close to the thirty-five miles an hour a whippet can attain, Dancer flashed past me and through the corner of the pasture before I even had time to react. Like a hound coursing a lure, eyes fixed on her prey, tail streaming behind her, she descended like the fury of Hades on that poor fox. If I hadn't shouted, I think she would have gotten him.

At first, I thought she had. There was a furious crashing of brush on the other side of the pasture fence and then a long, drawn-out snarling sound which was the whippet-pit bull curse: "*Missed him!*" Of course, I was screaming for her by that time, but it was useless. She tilted full-bore into the woods, vanishing from sight.

My initial fear was that she wouldn't come back. My second was that she would come back minus her coat, which would be snagged by one of several thousand trees. Once the fox made it to the woods, I didn't have too much fear for him. I had hunted too many foxes to think a single dog was going to take him in the woods. A pack, now, that was a different matter, or one large dog in the open. I thought Dancer was probably just going to give him the scare of his life.

Her self-satisfied expression when she returned several minutes later convinced me that she had. There was no blood on her muzzle and her coat was still on. I thought she had probably run him to ground in the old logging deadfall where he had made his den. She could dig there until the end of time and never get him out, but apparently she hadn't tried. "*Hunh, showed him,*" her face told me. "*Bet he won't come back soon.*"

He did, though. He came back almost every day, to taunt her. From that time on, though, he had his line of retreat figured out and Dancer never again got that close. It was pitched battle from which neither of them would retreat. There was nothing I could do about it and she always came back, so eventually I just let it be. It was good exercise for the dog.

Chapter Six

Exercise, ah, yes. Once upon a time, I had walked Polly. They were nice, sedate walks for the most part…times to meet the neighbors for a chat, to watch the occasional hawk sailing overhead or perched in a tree watching us, time to…Ach, dear Lord, what was that? *A CAT!* Now was the time to hope my shoulder wasn't dislocated from the force of a snarling menace hitting the end of the leash with every one of her increasing number of pounds.

Dancer throve on a diet of good food, warm snuggles pressed against my stomach under the covers at night, and exercise. I walked her on a fifteen-foot cotton web training lead because she was obsessed with smells. The dog sniffed her way along every roadside, path and hollow, nose so firmly pressed to the ground that I was surprised she didn't run headfirst into trees. She shredded those training leads in very short order and I had to keep buying more. Dancer was apparently on a quest to pursue every smell in my neighborhood and over 2,000 acres of adjacent State Game Lands. She had to be leashed there, it was the law, but there was no holding her on any six-foot, civilized, citified walking leash. No way. That dog could *MOVE*.

The only time I met neighbors now was when I flew by them. Sometimes, if it was early morning, I sailed past with a fixed grin, shouting, "Late for work, you know!" That was a best-case scenario. Worst-case scenario was if they had a dog with them.

I comprehended the gravity of such a situation the first time it happened. The dog was a Bernese Mountain Dog, a gentle black-and-tan giant being walked by a rather small girl he could have pulled over without effort. He was a gentleman, however, strolling along with his plume-like tail waving gently in the breeze, lips pulled pleasantly upwards in a sign of enjoyment. The dog and his owner both smiled at the sight of us and then I saw their expressions start to waver and disappear, like icing melting off a cake.

"Come on, come on, I can take him!" Dancer assured me, starting to accelerate. Head lowered, shoulders straining, she surged forward like a prize fighter readying the first punch. I hauled back on her choke collar, but she was undeterred. *"He's not so big. Come on, Mom, let's GO!"*

Dancer gave real meaning to the old expression, "It's not the size of the dog in the fight, it's the size of the fight in the dog." She made a noise somewhere between a whine, a snarl and a canine curse, assuring that dog she was going to have him for breakfast. He glanced at his owner uncertainly as we all heard

Dancer's toenails scraping furiously on the macadam. I hauled on the other end of the leash.

"No!" I admonished in my best dog-training voice. "No bite!"

It didn't work. That dog wasn't "mine." The noise Dancer was making continued up the scale, more threatening and feral with each passing moment. She pulled like a maniac, screaming dog curses. Finally, I took her by her collar, literally pinning her to the street so the girl and dog could pass us. They did, in a hurry.

"I'm sorry," I apologized, but the owner of the mountain dog wasn't sticking around for any niceties. Alas, my dog had just intensified the prejudice against half of her heritage.

Dancer had met the neighbors and adored every one, especially the children. She dearly loved to visit bus stops in the morning, offering her paws graciously to each youngster, never missing one. I had to keep her from going up the steps on the bus to join the children, who usually greeted her by name, waving from the windows.

But God help us if one of them had brought a dog. Then, she was the hound from hell. Then their mothers eyeballed her sideways, muttering among themselves that the dog actually was a pit bull, after all, and maybe they shouldn't really let their children near her. She practically foamed at the mouth. I must be crazy, having a dog like that. That was what one little boy assured me—

his mother had told him I was crazy.

The crazy lady and her dog took to walking up an old, abandoned railroad bed where very few people ever went. It was a perfect straightaway through woods, a gravel path just made for running. Dancer pulled so hard there that eventually I gave in and let her go.

It was like watching a greyhound. Legs flashing, belly low to the ground, she launched like something leaving a starting gate, eyes fixed on the horizon. From the rear, all I could see was her long black tail flying in the jet stream behind her. When she turned to come back (which she always did precisely when I would have gone out of sight), all I saw was her huge grin conveying both exuberance and a need for more air. When she stopped, her sides were always heaving but her eyes were shining with sheer exhilaration. The best thing in life, those eyes conveyed plainly, was to RUN! She quivered with the need for it, burned for it, challenged herself endlessly for one more burst of mindless, glorious speed before her radar went off and she turned back, reluctantly, because if she went any further she would be unable to see me. And that could never happen. God only knew what would become of us if she lost sight of me. I was her lifeline and she was mine.

No longer hampered by a dog whose heart was failing, who would lie down in the middle of even a short walk, I roamed for miles with Dancer-Dog. She was tireless. I never "got to the bottom" of that dog, as horse people say. I might return home exhausted, desperate for coffee to keep my floundering legs going, but Dancer was undeterred. Fueling herself with water lapped from roadside puddles, she just went on and on like the sorcerer's apprentice. It was like the dance of the magic brooms in "Fantasia." Polly had exhibited the same quality in her youth, interspersed with long periods of slumber, but Dancer never slept unless I insisted upon it. She still went outside every two hours all night if she could rouse me from my increasingly determined efforts to ignore her. I was growing weary and had lost about twenty pounds.

Still, I went on, clambering over hill and dale in the wake of a panting, happy dog. I had promised Dancer a good life and was determined to keep my word, even if I was having to bandage my toes because of their tendency to crack and bleed under the strain of forced marches. I just smiled when people congratulated me on my weight loss. If they only knew.

I asked my neighbors if I might run Dancer on the loose in their large field bordering the Game Lands. That way, I could follow at a more reasonable pace and still give the dog her exercise. Oh, sure, they said. They had a little nine-pound toy fox terrier just like Fred, and were die-hard dog lovers. The dog, Jill, visited Dancer through the fence and, oddly enough, was the one dog she liked.

Other dogs were still fair game. On one occasion I shudder to remember, Dancer didn't keep to the bounds of the field, crashing into the woods from which she could no longer see me. I couldn't believe it; she had never gone out of sight until that day. But she had spotted another neighbor's dog, a cute sheltie type named Gabriel. Gabriel had an attitude but no size to back it up and rolled like a ball, end over end, from the force of my dog simply running him down. She didn't bite, she just rolled him for his presumption in challenging her, and then trotted back to me with that self -satisfied expression I had seen the evening she routed Mr. Fox. *"Showed him,"* it said.

Thank God my neighbors were nice people. They only told me, reproachfully, that Gabriel had limped for a couple of days after that incident. I didn't want to deny Dancer the freedom of that field, which she needed very badly, so eventually I broke down and got her an electronic training collar. I knew she had real fear of my electric fence, even though she had run through it, and thought training her with electric shock was probably the only thing that would ever work.

I was right. It took only a couple of light zaps for her to understand how the collar worked. After that, simply pressing the button that gave her a warning beep turned her and she never again left the field. Any cat unlucky enough to come there while Dancer was coursing it was treed immediately, but pretty soon they knew when she was around and kept their distance. All the creatures including people gave us our space.

Chapter Seven

Much to Dancer's delight, it snowed. She was too low-slung to make much headway in the snow, so it was the one time I could turn her loose anywhere. She reveled in her newfound freedom, rising like a phoenix from the ashes of shelter existence. This was *LIFE*, her shining eyes and panting mouth seemed to say. She couldn't get enough of it.

It was still snowing on New Year's Day, lightly, the kind of snow that makes you simultaneously grateful for the comfort of a warm house and restless to go out and challenge the elements. Or at least I was. The cat, snuggled up on a dog-warmed pillow, wouldn't move, but the moment I picked up her long leash, Dancer was ready.

"Come on," I said. "We have an hour until dinner." The house was filling up with the smell of roasting chicken, but I knew once we were outside she would satisfy her appetites instead on the sharp scent of fresh snow and passing rabbits.

The road was covered enough to deter most drivers. In any case, I knew the majority of them would be home having the traditional pork and sauerkraut dinner almost everyone in the area seemed to make for New Year's. The only time I ever tried that, the shamrock on top of my Christmas tree had suddenly popped off and shot straight into the cat's litter box, which I took as a direct sign of displeasure from my Jewish grandparents. After that, I attempted to appease them for the Christmas tree by eating a nice Jewish chicken at New Year's. We would have it as soon as we returned. A short hop up and back on the old railroad bed took just about an hour.

We shuffled our way down a road filling with a light mixture of icy snow and I began to think that hour would be plenty. My fingers and toes were tingling, my breath was coming in short puffs so I didn't freeze my lungs. Dancer was well bundled in her fleecy coat and I knew as long as she was running she didn't seem to feel the cold, so I let her off the leash as we turned up the track. She took off so fast that I had to stifle a twinge of uneasiness when she disappeared on the path ahead of me. It was no day to get lost, so I whistled her back. She didn't come.

She always came. She never let me out of her sight and always came back—it was practically like religion. Where was my dog? I couldn't speed up on the slippery snow-covered rocks, but I whistled and called with a sense of growing urgency. I was just beginning to panic when I heard barking. It wasn't her playful bark nor her challenging one, it wasn't the joyous noise she made when she spotted a herd of deer and ran with them for a short distance, never biting but just apparently enjoying the race with kindred spirits. No, this was a short, staccato bark different from anything I had heard before and it didn't stop.

Ahead and to the right, a smaller track branched off, leading to a wooden footbridge over a small, deep creek. The barking seemed to be coming from there and I thought she had probably gone down for a drink. I was starting to get a little anxious about my chicken, so I called her again, but all I got was more barking. Drat, I would have to go get her. Turning onto the path, I spotted her standing on the bridge beside a dark, hairy lump. Oh, Lord, she had found something dead. I just hoped she wasn't rolling in it. She was licking it as if thinking about it.

"Dancer!" I hollered, not anxious to have a reeking dog I'd somehow have to bathe in freezing weather. She looked up at me and that's when I saw it wasn't dead. Dancer, the dog who hated other dogs, was licking the face of a dog lying on the bridge. Wait...no...not ON the bridge. He was IN the bridge. Incredulous, I realized that all four of his legs had somehow gone through the slats and he was stuck there like a cork in a bottle, unable to extricate himself.

"Oh, my God." I slid on my knees beside the barely-breathing lump of old, frozen, snow-covered dog. He had a thick coat like a shepherd mix, but even so rivulets of water and ice were running in ropey snarls down his sides. His face was snowy and it was that snow Dancer was licking off him.

I guess he might have bitten me, but I never thought about it. All I could think was that this dog was going to die—soon. Levering myself down, I tried to slide my hands through the slats to free his legs, but it was pointless. He was frozen stiff, unable to move a leg even if I had been able to work it free, and he looked like a good ninety pounds. I wasn't going to be able to lift him out. I looked around in vain for help, but of course there was nobody. Nobody there.

As quickly as I could, I pulled off my parka and wrapped it around the unmoving dogs, securing the sides beneath him. He didn't even react, he was so far gone.

"Don't move, buddy," I told him. "Hang on, I'm going to get you some help. I'll be back." I stood up, not knowing if Dancer would follow, but she didn't move. "Stay there, girl," I said, "he needs you."

Dancer, the dog who hated other dogs and never let me out of her sight, stood like a rock as I took off as fast as possible back down the trail, down the road, to where my friends Pat and Denise lived. I was practically sobbing with relief when I saw chimney smoke from their woodstove. If it was burning, they were home. I pounded on the door.

Pat answered, with Denise right behind him because,

looking at me, they couldn't doubt there was trouble.

"I need help," I said. "There's an old dog stuck in the slats of the bridge back in the woods. He looks like he's dying and I can't get him out."

Denise was already grabbing a spare coat for me. The trail wasn't wide enough to take Pat's big truck and we would have to go in on foot, carrying blankets and ropes and whatever else we thought would be needed.

"He's a big dog," I told them. "I think it's going to take more than us to get him out."

"Probably," Pat agreed. "I'll take my chainsaw and come with you. Denise, call the fire company."

Our volunteer fire company was probably eating pork and sauerkraut that minute. I didn't even want to think about my chicken. I figured they might be putting hoses on my house along about the time they got that dog out, but I puffed my way back into the woods anyway with Pat, several blankets and a chain saw.

Dancer was still there, still licking the frozen dog. He didn't look any better. I thought it would be a miracle if he lived, even if we could get him out.

"No, this is going to take a crew," Pat said, lifting my coat off the dog and replacing it with blankets. He handed it to me. "Go turn off your oven and come back. I'll stay with him." We had no doubt the fire company would come. We knew most of those guys and they always came, holiday or not.

I really was worried about my house by then, so much as I hated to do it, I called Dancer. Apparently she thought her job was done, because she followed me without hesitation and we fled at top speed up the road just in time to keep the chicken from incinerating.

"You are a GOOD dog," I told her, cupping her chin and looking her in the eyes. "You knew that old boy needed help, didn't you?" She just wagged her tail and lapped my wrist with her tongue.

"I'm gonna go see if he's all right," I told her. "You stay and take care of the chicken."

She would have taken care of that chicken, except I'd left it in the oven, now turned off. It was probably a lost cause, but I had to know what happened to the dog. This time, though, I took my truck.

It looked like a truck convention at the entrance to the old path. Pickups, a pumper and an ambulance. Ambulance? There were a couple of frantic-looking people who weren't firemen bolting up the path and a bunch of volunteer firemen coming out in a small-sized pickup. The dog was lying wrapped in blankets in the bed of the truck, with an oxygen mask over his face and a bunch of firemen leaning over him.

Denise met us at the entrance, where I handed her coat

back to her. She gestured at the couple I'd seen running towards the bridge, now climbing into the back of the truck.

"Those are his owners," she said. "They'd reported him missing at the SPCA." I knew she was responsible for the assemblage of help. No doubt she'd been a busy girl on the phone while Pat and I were with the dog.

"How is he?" I asked, and she shook her head. Between us, we had cared for more pets and livestock than ten people, and not all of them had lived.

"They called their vet and he's opening his office for them," she said. They're going to take him." I could see by her expression she also thought the dog was going to die. Still, we had done what we could. "I gave them my number. Maybe they'll let us know how he is."

They were transferring the dog into the back of their SUV even as we spoke. "He went missing a couple of days ago," Denise said. "He's old and wandered out of the yard. They've been looking everywhere for him."

Everywhere but in the woods, I thought, but I knew in my heart if Dancer hadn't found him, no one would have. God knew how long he had been there, helpless and freezing. Even if they couldn't save him, at least he wouldn't die that way.

"How in the world did you spot him?" she asked.

"I didn't. Dancer found him. I was walking her and she

took off running, and then I heard her barking, so I went to look."

"Wow, yeah, they know."

"They do," I agreed. How she had known, of course, was beyond me. Still, as Denise, said, dogs just did.

"I wonder if we'll ever hear from them," I speculated, watching the taillights of the owners' car disappearing, in the snow and in a hurry.

My friend was a realist. "Probably not."

She was right, we never did. But the chicken was still chewable and Dancer got a very full plate. That night she curled up against me in her head-tucked, whippet legs-folded position, snoring softly. Stroking her hard little head and rose-petal ears, I thought about the old dog. Sometimes I felt that way—alone, out in the cold, stuck in a place where I couldn't move.

But I had Dancer. She needed me. I needed her. We were a team. And we would make it.

AFTERWORD

These were only a few of our adventures. For another nine years, Dancer and I made it together in our little place in time. Eventually there was a second dog, a black Lab pup who became her other world.

Our dogs never live long enough, and Dancer was no exception. Time, and perhaps the hard life she had lived before she came to me, took their toll. When there was no more I could do for her, she died in my arms.

She lives on today in the many other dogs I have taken into my heart and into my home. It's getting hard to remember all of them, but there was Kipsy who narrowly avoided being put to death. Dudley, lost or abandoned in the mountains of North Carolina and then consigned to a kill shelter where he was just another unwanted hound, until a volunteer spotted him and posted on Facebook for help. Home Free Rescue and I were the ones who answered.

There was little Mushie who was going to be killed at six weeks of age. She is with me still, as is Teddy the black Lab. He is an old man now, dreaming happy dreams on his dog bed in my office. There was Tia, my beautiful golden pit bull, so much like Dancer. And Delilah, whose mother and litter were delivered by a kind trucker to a local rescue. They are only some of the many, but together we can save them all.

Everybody deserves to be rescued.

www.ingramcontent.com/pod-product-compliance
Lightning Source LLC
Chambersburg PA
CBHW021224020426
42331CB00003B/465